KING RENÉ'S

BOOK OF LOVE

KING RENÉ'S BOOK OF LOVE

BOOK OF LOVE

(Le Cueur d'Amours Espris)

THE NATIONAL LIBRARY, VIENNA

INTRODUCTION AND COMMENTARIES BY

F. UNTERKIRCHER

GEORGE BRAZILLER   NEW YORK

Reproduced from the Illuminated Manuscript (Cod. Vind. 2597)
Belonging to the Austrian National Library in Vienna.

Translated from the German by Sophie Wilkins

Published in 1975

Library of Congress Catalog Card Number: 75-7957
International Standard Book Number: 0-8076-0788-6

Printed in Austria by Akademische Druck-u. Verlagsanstalt
BOOK DESIGN BY VINCENT TORRE
SLIPCASE AND BINDING DESIGN BY OSCAR RATTI

CONTENTS

INTRODUCTION

ONCE UPON A TIME—the story could begin, just as in a fairy tale—over five hundred years ago, there was a King of Sicily and Duke of Anjou who was called Good King René. His subjects loved him because he knew how to secure their prosperity, and they did not begrudge him the many splendid castles he owned throughout his lands, nor the gay parties and entertainments he gave there. But one of these castles was also a favorite retreat for himself and his young wife whenever he wanted to withdraw to write his books in peaceful surroundings. For he was not only a king, but the author of stories about knighthood, intrepid journeys in search of adventure, heroic deeds, and the human heart's loves and sorrows. To help his readers understand his words all the better, his books were illustrated with paintings so lively and skillful that their beauty still lives today.

Much of this fairy tale is historic fact, particularly the paintings in the books of René, and a sequence of sixteen illuminated folios from his principal work is reproduced here. If they are to be understood, the persons and events of the fairy tale underlying them must be moved into the light of historical reality.

Duke René of Anjou played a most impressive part in the stormy history of fifteenth-century France and Italy. He was the son and third child of Duke Louis II of Anjou and Yolande of Aragon, born on January 16, 1409, in their castle at Angers in the Maine-and-Loire region of western France. A brother, Louis, had been born in 1403, and his sister Maria (who was to marry Charles VI of France), in 1404. René grew up in Anjou and in Provence, another of his father's domains. In 1419 the ten-year-old was married to Isabel of Lorraine, who was only nine. Such youthful dynastic marriages were frequently resorted to in those days, as effective weapons in the constant struggles for power (whether on the level of diplomatic accommodation or ruthless warfare) in the course of which today's allies all too frequently became tomorrow's bloodthirsty enemies.

Duke Charles of Lorraine, René's father-in-law, was at war with King Charles VII of France who was also involved in the Hundred-Years War with England. England's ally in this war was the powerful Duke of Burgundy, Philip the Good. René, when old enough to bear arms, joined the forces—including Joan of Arc— who were fighting for the King of France. When his father-in-law died in 1431 René inherited the Duchy of Lorraine. But a nephew of the deceased Duke also laid claim to this inheritance, with armed assistance from the Duke of Burgundy. That same year the contending parties met in battle at Bulignéville, where René was defeated and captured. Duke Philip of Burgundy asserted his right to the valuable prisoner and took René to his fortress at Dijon.

During René's imprisonment his young wife Isabel proved to be a most skillful advocate on his behalf. She even succeeded in obtaining René's temporary release from his dungeon, on his word of honor to return at the stipulated time (which he doubly guaranteed by leaving his two young children behind as hostages in Dijon). René remained at liberty for three years but returned to the Dijon fortress in 1435, to wait there for another year before the Duke of Burgundy finally gave him his freedom in return for a substantial ransom.

René's interest in painting seems to date from the time of his incarceration at Dijon, where, it is said, he occupied himself with painting on glass and decorated one of the rooms in the castle. None of this work has survived, but there is a prayerbook of René's from this period with a number of illuminations that already show some characteristics of his later style. There is also a legend to the effect that, at Dijon, René met the Dutch painter Jan van Eyck and became his pupil. Since van Eyck was employed in the service of the Duke of Burgundy at the time, this is a possibility. It may be a point where fairy tale and reality converge.

But reality now took a firm grip on René. His elder brother Louis had died in 1434, so that René now became the Duke of

Anjou. In addition to the Duchy, his brother had bequeathed him a royal crown, for Queen Joan of Naples and Sicily had made Louis of Anjou her Co-Regent and heir and, after Louis's death, named René as his brother's heir. In 1435 Joan died while René was still imprisoned at Dijon. His wife Isabel must be credited not only with safeguarding his rights to Lorraine, Anjou, and Provence, but also with actively representing his claim to Naples and Sicily against Alfonso of Aragon's counterclaim. It finally became necessary for René to betake himself to his new kingdom in person. In the spring of 1438 he journeyed from Marseille to Genoa, an ally, and thence to Naples where he was joyfully received.

There followed four years of changing fortunes. His peaceful reign in Naples was constantly interrupted by battles with Alfonso, fought at various points in southern Italy. In the summer of 1442, René was forced to abandon Naples. For a time he sojourned in Florence and northern Italy, but in the fall of that year he returned to Provence. Thereafter, he was King of Sicily in name only.

He was now all the more able to devote himself successfully to ruling his French territories and, with these as his base, participate in the Renaissance game of high politics. His oldest son, John of Calabria, would continue to fight for the South-Italian kingdom; his daughter Marguerite married King Henry VI of England in 1445; his younger daughter Yolande and her husband had been given the Duchy of Lorraine. René's relations with his brother-in-law, Charles VII, were so harmonious that the French king even found his legendary love, Agnes Sorel, at René's court—she was one of Isabel of Anjou's ladies.

Those years of nearly unbroken peace from 1442 to 1453 presented, at last, an opportunity for the unfolding of the rituals of a princely household. Court was held at René's and Isabel's castles throughout Anjou and Provence, many of which had been newly restored and refurbished. Saumur on the Loire, cited in René's principal work as the very model of a fine castle, became the family's favorite residence. It is during this peaceful decade that reality and fairy tale become difficult to separate: the wise administration of René's domains is historical fact, while the romantic surroundings René created for his court have the aura of a fairy tale. It was the world of such knightly romances as the legends of the Holy

Grail, of King Arthur's Round Table, of Tristan and Iseult, of the nine heroic knights. It was with such characters as these that the knights of the fifteenth century identified, and their world revolved around such concepts as might be found in the witty allegories of the *Romance of the Rose*, their classic love breviary. In addition to the usual festive gatherings at the various castles and the great mystery plays to which the public was welcome, the crowning occasions of knightly activity in peacetime were, of course, the great tourneys. René was tireless in arranging for these scenes of knightly combat, some of which (as with the great tourneys at Nancy and Tarascon) enjoyed such fame that they were immortalized by the poets.

His first book, in fact, was *The Manual for the Perfect Organization of Tourneys*, an actual handbook, and indeed no one was a better-qualified author. It was prepared during the late 1440s, about the time René's great tourneys were actually held. When it was reported to René that a noble lord of high degree had expressed himself disparagingly about the Duke of Anjou's new literary activity, saying: "It ill befits a prince to descend to such scribbler's work," René's comment was: "Such words might come more fittingly from a bellowing bull than a noble prince."

In all his undertakings, whether they concerned the sober administration of government business or the festive life of a knightly dream world, Isabel was Rene's helpmate. When death took his wife from him in 1453, he was inconsolable. His deep mourning for her may have played a part in his letting himself be persuaded to go to war in Italy once more, on behalf of his old claim to the throne of Naples and Sicily. Florence and Milan, fighting against Alfonso of Aragon (then ruling Naples), called upon the King of France for aid; he sent them Duke René in his stead. In midsummer of 1453 René went to Italy, but he returned to France in February 1454 though the Italian campaign had not yet been decided one way or the other.

For René, the time of battles and political ambitions was now over. His second wife, whom he married in September 1454 in Angers, was Jeanne of Laval, the daughter of a Breton nobleman. She was twenty-four years younger than René, who was just forty-five. Again, that fairy-tale element in the story: the King secluded with his young wife in the quiet castle, writing and illustrating his books. For René actually stayed at Angers and at Saumur, where his literary works came into being, almost uninterruptedly until 1471. Then he moved to Provence, taking his entire, carefully inventoried library with him. He died at Aix-la-Chappelle on July 10, 1480.

René had provided for a fitting tombstone at the Church of Saint Maurice in Angers during his lifetime. Above the marble tomb was affixed one of his own large paintings, showing a dying king on a throne. The figure, holding scepter and orb, is halfway to being a skeleton already, his crown threatening to slip off the head leaning to one side. This memorial was destroyed during the French Revolution. But the memory of Good King René is preserved in history and literature, not least by his own works.

Though his manual for conducting tournaments was a work of practical instruction in armed combat, his subsequent books were purely literary. The first two dealt with widely divergent subject matter: one was a pastoral love poem, the other a mystical dialogue about the vanity of all earthly things. The poem, *Regnault et Jeanneton* (created in 1454–55), about the love of a shepherd and shepherdess whose fictional names hardly disguise the fact that they stand for René and Jeanne, was a bridal gift to the author's young second wife. It was succeeded not much later by *The Mortification of Vain Pleasure (Le Mortifiement de Vaine Plaisance)*, a dialogue carried on by the allegorical figures Fear of God *(Crainte de Dieu)*, Love of God *(Souverain Amour)*, Remorse *(Contrition)*, Faith *(Ferme-Foy)*, and Grace of God *(Grace Divine)*, regarding the love of God as being the way to purge the soul of all earthly folly. We are sure of the date, although it does make the work seem oddly timed. Such thoughts might have been expected to arise immediately after the death of Isabel rather than after René's second marriage. But the months of warfare in Italy would hardly have provided the opportunity for creating such a work. We may certainly conjecture, therefore, that the plan for it originated during his time of deep mourning, though it was not completed until somewhat later under more favorable circumstances.

These two lesser efforts were followed immediately by René's masterpiece, *Le Livre du Cueur d'Amours Espris*, in 1457. This book of the heart as love's captive is a direct descendant of the classic *Romance of the Rose*, with its allegorical characters clearly

(11)

labeled by names indicating their natures and functions. Although such a world of personified abstractions may not be too congenial to modern modes of thinking, René's contemporaries were quite comfortable with it. It was, in fact, a popular scenario for the literature of the period.

René's allegorical romance is presented within a rather circumscribed "realistic" frame. He tells us that he went to bed early one night, tired and preoccupied with musings about love. Then—was it a vision, a dream?—Love himself suddenly appears before him, taking the heart from his breast and handing it to Desire. This is where the story begins. At its end, René awakens in terror, clutching his left breast—his heart, did Love really take it? He cries out for his valet, by the light of whose candle they reassure themselves that the left side of his chest is whole and undamaged. Greatly relieved, René happily takes paper and pen to record his dream.

The Heart, represented in the dream as a knight in full armor named Cueur (or Cuer), accompanied by his Page, Desire, sets off on a perilous journey of courtship to liberate Sweet Grace (*Dame Doulce-Mercy*), who is being held in captivity by three enemies of Love: Denial (*Reffus*), Shame (*Honte*), and Fear (*Crainte*). Only the first part of the journey is illustrated by the sixteen paintings in the Vienna manuscript. The last of these portrays an intermediate landing, by night, on a rocky island. The story, however, goes on from that point, telling of the next morning, when the companions reembark for the rest of the voyage until, late that evening, they reach the Island of Love, There, in the moonlight, they behold Love's marvelous castle; nearby is the *Hospital d'Amours*. The visitors are welcomed kindly by Compassion (*Pitié*), the hospital's prioress, who shows them around the spacious building. Its sickrooms are occupied by all the famed lovers of history (as well as of their own day), such as Paris, Theseus, Hercules, Caesar, Augustus, Nero, Tristan, Lancelot, Charles of Orleans, Gaston Foix, Charles VII of France, and a certain René of Anjou, a close acquaintance of Cueur's. In a garden behind the hospital is Love's cemetery, holding the graves of the great poets of love, Ovid, Petrarch, Boccaccio, and many more.

The next day the guests are received at the Chateau of Pleasure (*Chateau de Plaisance*) by the young God of Love, Amour, and his mother, Venus. All the beauties of this castle, which resembles the Castle of Saumur, are described in great detail, including ten tapestries in the great hall, eight tapestries in Venus's bedchamber, and the deer park with its exotic beasts and creatures of fable. Cueur receives permission from the God of Love to release Sweet Grace from her confinement in the Fortress of Resistance (*Manoir de Rebellion*). Cueur and his companions manage to enter the fortress without resorting to violence. The last-ditch resistance of Denial is overcome by Generosity, who tosses him two purses filled with gold. Sweet Grace, meanwhile, has been apprised of Cueur's impending arrival by Compassion and Welcome, and gracefully accepts his homage. But it is only after Shame and Fear have been driven away that Cueur manages to coax the first kiss from his lady's lips. Accompanied by Desire, Modest Plea, and Compassion, he then sets out with Sweet Grace for the Chateau of Pleasure. But on the way they are ambushed by all the enemies of Love. Desire is killed, Cueur gravely wounded, Sweet Grace recaptured. Compassion then takes Cueur into her charge. She comforts him as best she can, but she has to warn him that he must think no more of Sweet Grace, doomed to remain forever in the power of Denial. Cueur allows Compassion to take him to the *Hospital d'Amours*, where he expects to end his days in prayer and silent remembrance.

This bittersweet love story is spun out most artfully and circumstantially by the author. The prose passages of the narrative are continually interspersed with long passages in verse, the thoughts and words of the characters, and inscriptions along the way, displaying the author's admirable learning in history and mythology, as well as his skill in the invention of allegorical figures. Dames Fantasy and Imagination, credited with the splendors of Love's castle, are René's best assistants. He not only had eyes receptive to the marvels of nature, but the gift of describing them most evocatively. His work celebrates the bright greens of meadows and hills, the darker hues of forests, the twittering of the birds in the trees, and, above all, the light in all its infinite variations: the rising sun at dawn; the shimmering daylight over the landscape and the sea; the sinking of the evening sun; dusk; and blackest night under the glittering stars.

The poet, in fact, seems to be walking hand in hand with the painter—or was he the painter as well? In addition to the sixteen illuminations we have, space for twenty-nine more had been re-

(13)

served. There is another manuscript of this work where all of the paintings have been completed, but it is a later manuscript and its painter nowhere approaches the virtuosity of the *Cueur* Master.

It is for art historians to solve the riddles posed by the Master of the Vienna *Cueur*, which is a crowning achievement not only of French book illumination, but of book illumination in general. The painter was not satisfied merely to represent objects and figures in glowing color; he created a palpable atmosphere which gives life to everything contained on the page, whether nature's mood by day or night, or the characters in the story.

King René had numerous artists in his employ, decorating his castles, creating his tapestries, completing the paintings he commissioned. Among the many names of such artists on record, the most likely *Cueur* Master would have been a certain Barthelemy de Cler (or Deick), according to Provençal documents. He was a close friend of René's, in touch with him from 1447 to 1478. But there is an ancient tradition that holds René himself to have been a master painter. It is said that he taught himself to paint during the years he spent in the Tower of Dijon and continued to practice his art thereafter. The sixteen paintings of the Vienna manuscript were created during the latter half of the 1460s, that peaceful period when René lived at Saumur, in Anjou. There he would also have had the leisure to begin work on the illustrations for his masterwork, for which a professional calligrapher had executed the text.

* * * *

There are six manuscripts extant of *Le Cueur d'Amours Espris* (also known as *Le Cuer d'Amours Espris* or *Le Coeur d'Amour Epris*). Five date from the end of the fifteenth century— four in Paris (three at the Bibliothèque Nationale, one in the Bibliothèque d'Arsenal) and one in the Vatican Library. The sixth is the manuscript in the Austrian National Library, Vienna: Cod. Vind. 2597. This is the oldest and also the most beautiful, being the only one illuminated by the *Cueur* Master. The original manuscript is 127 parchment pages in length, each page measuring 290 x 207 mm. It was originally acquired by the Austrian national hero, Prince Eugene of Savoy; we do not know how or from whom. As part of Prince Eugene's library, it became one of the treasures of the Austrian Imperial Library in 1736.

PLATES AND COMMENTARIES

René, the King and Poet, is asleep. In a magical night scene he sees himself and the figures in his dream: Amour, God of Love, is standing beside his bed and with both hands plucks the heart from René's breast, giving it to the Page, Ardent Desire, who stands with hands outstretched ready to receive it. It will have to remain in the power of Ardent Desire until it finds favor with the lady of René's dreams, Sweet Grace. It is not René himself who starts off on a journey of adventure with the Page, but his heart, personified as the Knight Cueur.

The artist brings this multileveled poetic allegory to life by giving its characters a three-dimensional reality and endowing the scenes with color shadings and light that almost transcend reality, suggesting that realm between dream and daylight wherein poetry has its roots.

The scene is a princely bedchamber, its floor entirely covered by a mat woven Egyptian style, topped with two costly Persian rugs. The tapestry on the rear wall shows a pattern of stylized tree trunks, echoed in the upper border of the canopy, with curtains in heavy, gathered folds around the bed. The page's low cot at the right has a conical tent for a canopy. A low-burning candle beneath the simple bench at the foot of this cot modestly lights the scene from below. Thus the brightest light falls upon the Page Desire in his handsome white court dress, the skirt of his pleated tunic embroidered with red-and-yellow flames. Also well lighted is the handsome face of Amour, turned toward Desire. The God of Love's wings are blue-green; he is wearing a blue Oriental tunic with broad golden borders interwoven with an ancient Arabic script. His bow and arrows, in a richly decorated Oriental quiver, are at his left side. The King's face is mostly in shadow, his white bed linen catching most of the light. Strong shadows are cast by the legs of Amour and Desire. The painting's physical details are as easy to describe as it is difficult or impossible to do justice in words to its rich, dreamy atmosphere and masterful color harmonies.

Cte nuyt en ce mois passe
Trauaille tourmente lasse
Fforment pensifz ou lit me mis
Comme homme lais qui A si mis
Son cueur en la mercy damours
Que ma vie en plains et en plours

Like those knights who went in quest of the Holy Grail, Cueur has now set out with his Page Desire to win the loveliest of ladies, Sweet Grace. Encased in heavy armor, his face invisible behind the closed visor of his helmet which is crowned with a winged heart encircled by a wreath of pansies *(amoureuses pensées* or loving thoughts), his shield bearing a device of three forget-me-nots, Cueur carries gifts *(dons)* on the sharp point of his cypress-wood lance, with which to conquer the enemies of Love. He rides the steed Candor *(Franc Vouloir)*, spurred on by love's remembrance *(d'amoureux souvenir)*. The horse's saddlecloth is embroidered with winged hearts.

Here the two men have just emerged onto a grassy plain from a deep forest, in an unknown country. Under a pine tree stands a tent, wondrous and lovely to behold, guarded by a rectangular column of jasper which is inscribed as follows:

> Oh ye noble and engaging hearts, longing to win sweet favors and joyful gratitude from the God of Love and your Lady, do not waver in your resolution, never abandon your first love but be true to her, unchanging from one day to the next. . . .

A lady has come out of the tent and stands before them, holding the reins of Cueur's horse. She is no longer young, but of noble bearing, royally clad, and wearing a golden crown. She tells Cueur that her name is Hope *(Esperance)*, that Amour himself ordered the inscription on that column to guide all lovers on their quest, and gives him encouragement concerning the road ahead. He will have to withstand many battles, but he will always be able to count on her aid.

This scene takes place in broad daylight, with all the details—pine branches, richly embroidered borders on the tent, costumes—lovingly executed. The painting is a model of composition with text and illustration blended into a perfect whole on one book page: an objectively motivated upward extension of the picture on the left takes the place of the decorative framework, balanced by a similar projection on the right of the next folio.

voulsist ou non si durement sestoit ladicte dame desa bride saisie
Doncques quant Il vit cela si descendit apie et salua la da
me en luy demandant et priant quil luy pleust de luy dire qui
elle estoit ne pourquoy lauoit ainsi arreste / Et dit en
telle maniere

Dame pour dieu que or vous plaise
Pour mon vouloir mettre a son aise
Amor dire las de vostre estre
Car sur toutes me samblez estre

After days of crossing plains, hills, and forests, Cueur and Desire finally emerge from one of the most sinister and terrifying forests ever known (seen at left) to find themselves before the chapel of a hermitage. With its arched entrance, three-cornered gable, and belfry, it is twelfth-century Provençal in style. As though blocking the entrance to this sanctuary there stands a female dwarf who is ugliness personified. Wild strands of hair stand up on her head, and she has piercing eyes as well as a venomous glance. Her nose is misshapen and her mouth stretches from ear to huge, hanging ear. Below her darkly repellent forehead and face the shoulders and hips are malformed, and one low-hanging udder is visible. Hairy arms and legs scratched by thorns and the broad, clumsy feet of a swan (barely covered by the two lion skins which are clumsily knotted together over her shoulders) complete the picture. The description of this gargoyle in the text is even less flattering than the artist's portrait. She is Jealousy *(Jalousie)*, Love's sworn enemy. Amour had actually sent the handsome boy Welcome *(Bel Accueil)* to meet Cueur and Desire as their messenger and guide, but Jealousy has ambushed him and locked him up.

Desire politely asks Jealousy for a night's lodging, but the hideous dwarf answers him with only shrill hostility and curses. Cueur longs to kill her on the spot, but Desire stops him—she is, after all, a woman, and there would be little honor in such a deed. Accordingly, Cueur restrains himself and asks her for directions. Jealousy tells them how to reach the Castle of Good Rest *(Bon Repos)*, but in reality she is sending the two men, with malice aforethought, on a false trail into the Forest of the Long Wait *(Le Forest de Longue-Attente)*.

In the illustration, the malicious dwarf takes up relatively little space. The dominant figure is that of Desire, clad in white, behind whom the forest stretches back into mysterious darkness. In effective contrast to this we have the bright facade of the chapel, with its lovingly detailed decorations, and the blue sky above it (on the right). In this predominantly benign atmosphere the only unpleasant note is struck by the ugliness of Jealousy.

poil nouces sur lespaule Et bien resembloit creature pou cour
toise malgracieuse despite et pou amoureuse lors sauanca de
sir li damnseaulx comme celur qui bien cuidoit sauoir la lan
gue et le paye et parla ala narne en telle maniere

Tien ça narne se dieu te sault
Pour ce que le Jour nous deffault
Demande alermite leans
Se pourrons herbergier ceans

Here is a night scene such as had never before been attempted in manuscript illumination, executed with a virtuosity hardly equaled even afterward. At the center, Cueur and Desire are resting under an aspen tree. Cueur has doffed his helmet so that his face is visible in three-quarter profile; his armor gleams in the dusk. At left, the horses are grazing, Cueur's tall saddle outlined against the starry sky. At right, a tall dark slab can be seen, and more stars shimmer between the slender trees.

From the text we learn that after long wanderings, astray in the Forest of the Long Wait, Cueur and Desire finally emerged from the woods at nightfall. In the dark they came upon a broad marble slab with a fresh-water spring at its foot and a shallow brass cup on a chain resting on top. Although they cannot see how pure the water may be, Desire takes a drink, then hands the cup to Cueur who, after drinking from it, carelessly lets the rest of the water run down the marble shaft. Instantly, the hitherto clear, starry sky grows overcast with heavy storm-clouds; thunder and lightning, rain and hail come hurtling down on the helplessly exposed men, drenching them before they can reach shelter under a trembling aspen tree, they themselves trembling and shivering. The storm ends as suddenly as it began, and the stars shine through the trees once more. The men are shown resting, Cueur propped up on his right hand, Desire leaning on his left elbow, talking over the fright they have just had, before they fall asleep. It is not until the next morning that they will find the solution to this mystery.

venir aual et ciel et nuees et les deux compaignons auc
ques espouentez & lorriblete du temps se retrahirent/
Incontinent soubz le tramble et se misdrent alabry le
mieulx quilz sceurent/ Mais tout ce ne leur valut riens
quilz ne fussent tresbien baignez et froissiez de la pluye
et de lagresle quilz sembloient estre retrau du fons dune
riviere Si doubta adonc desir que le cueur ne fust re
boute de son emprise car asses ennuyeuse estoit sa pre
miere rencontre si ne se peult plus tenir quil ne parlast
aluy et luy dist en telle maniere

The sun, encircled by a shimmering aureole, rises behind a tall hedge on the horizon to herald the dawn of a new day. The bright light it casts on the meadow with its finely detailed grasses is emphasized by the long shadows cast by the hedge. Cueur is standing in front of the marble slab, gravely reading the inscription which he had not been able to see the night before:

> Beneath this marble shaft, as black as coal rises the Spring of Chance.* He who drinks of it will suffer dire misery. For this spring was brought forth by the sorcerer Vergil, who laid his curse upon it. A little of its water, poured on this marble shaft, will instantly unleash a raging storm. . . .

Thus the answer to the fearsome riddle of the night before. Cueur then sees for the first time that the water, issuing from a lion's head near the base of the shaft, looks foul and revolting; never would he have drunk it had he seen it first. This baneful spring flows on to become a brook, a Stream of Tears which Cueur and Desire will encounter repeatedly as they journey onward.

The grim inscription, prophesying misery and danger ahead, is the one black note in a painting otherwise expressive only of the radiance of a joyful new morning. And the black marble does not prevail against the glorious colors unfolding around it: the blue of the sky, brightening nearer the sun, the yellow-ish green of the meadow, the reddish brown of the horse with its silver mane and tail, the tree trunks gleaming in the sun, the wood-tones of the lance, all interspersed with sharp morning shadows.

The final touch in this composition is provided by the figures of the two men: at the right, Cueur in armor but without his helmet, his left hand extended as he follows the lines of the inscription, his face aware and thoughtful. The red of his cap is echoed on the left by the red heart on his helmet, the embroidered hearts on his horse's saddlecloth, the red straps of his shield. On this bright young morning, already shadowed by the heavy cares and anxieties evoked by the black marble slab with its inscription and foul spring, all desire lies dormant—Desire lies fast asleep under the aspen tree, his right hand supporting his head with its sorrowful look, his left hand, relaxed in sleep, on his knee.

This peaceful morning will be followed by a trying day, and more to come.

*La Fontaine de Fortune—but fortune in its negative, shifting, treacherous aspects.

Droit cy deuant soubz ce perron
De marbre noir comme charbon
Sourt la fontaine de fortune
Ou il nya quelle nesune
Et la fist compasser et faire
Ung tyrant Joyant de fauly assaire

After following the little Stream of Tears from the Spring of Chance, Cueur and Desire enter a broad valley in a deserted region. Here, on the bank of the muddy stream, they find a dilapidated hut roofed with straw. An inscription above the low doorway reads:

> This wide and frightening valley is called by all men the Valley of Deepest Thoughts. Here in this hut lives Melancholy, no man's friend.

Desire remains on his horse, while Cueur has dismounted, leaving his lance leaning against his handsome saddle. To enter the hut he must bend low. Through a wide window on the side facing the viewer, Dame Melancholy can be seen—a lamentable figure of a woman all in black, trying to warm her hands over a tiny fire. Cueur politely asks her for a little bread for himself and his companion. She tosses him a piece of gray bread, not out of compassion but because she knows that this bread has never yet agreed with whomever ate it, for it is made of a grain called Hard Want, mixed with water from the Stream of Tears. But the travelers are so famished by now that they eat it nonetheless, quenching their thirst with the muddy water from the Stream of Tears. In the end, Melancholy agrees to show them on their way.

Again, the painting does not quite express the despair it is supposed to illustrate. The hut is not shown surrounded by a thorny thicket, as described, nor does it look dilapidated with its neat and solid thatched roof, despite the few cracks in the masonry between the timbers. The figure of Melancholy in her dark gown, with her long flowing hair, delicate hands, and woefully upturned eyes, compels admiration. As a forceful counterpoint to Melancholy, toward whom Cueur is inclined, there is Desire at the left, watching him with some concern but on the whole a figure of strength and unbroken vitality. The lively colors at the left, whence a narrow strip of blue sky extends even over the roof of Melancholy's home, appears to promise a victory of desire over dark mournfulness in the end.

qui estoit si petit que apaine y eust sceu ung chat bruler sa
queue Et vit une grant vielle escheuelee morne et pensiue qui
seoit au pres du fouier et tenoit ses mains ensamble maigre
et ridee estoit terriblement Et ale vous abregier Il sambloit
quelle fust retraitte de terre car oncques home ne vit plus orri
ble ne plus espouentable creature Et se pensa bien que cestoit
celle melencolie dont le tableau qui estoit sur lure de la maison
nette parloit Si la salua lecuer mais apame luy rendit elle
son salut car trop durement pensoit ailleurs Touteffois Il
ne se tint pas atant mais parla a elle et dist ainsi

Melancholy has led the knight and his page along the Stream of Tears until they find themselves before the bridge called Dangerous Crossing *(Pas Peril-leux)*. It is an old wooden bridge supported by a primitive structure of wooden posts, with a steep ascent and broken planks, so narrow that there is barely room for a single horse. The riverbank is crumbling, undermined by the stream, so that the bridge appears liable to collapse at any moment. Melancholy has led the two travelers hither not out of kindness but because she knew that, soon enough, they would have little joy of it. She is, in fact, already pointing to the opposite bank, where a Black Knight approaches. Black is his armor, his lance, his horse and all its paraphernalia—all but the yellow of three marigolds (*soussye-souci*—sorrow), which form the device on his shield, and the bunch of columbines (*aquilegia-ancoly*—melancholy) on his helmet. It is the Knight Soucy (Trouble, Anxiety) who guards this bridge against all lovers.

Here too the grim aspect of the Black Knight and Dame Melancholy, visually linked by the dark bridge of peril, is softened by the loveliness of the landscape with its many gradations of green over meadows, trees, and bushes, paling on the heights and in the distance, as well as the blue-white of the lightly clouded sky. There are also the bright colors in the left foreground: Desire's white clothing with its golden flame pattern, his red-brown horse standing still, its eyes looking out of the picture, the red hearts on Cueur's helmet and saddlecloth, the red edging of his saddle. The two kinds of spurs are clearly distinguished: Cueur's end in a prod, Desire's in a rowel. In contrast to the immobile Page on his quiet horse, Cueur prepares to attack. His horse has already lifted one foreleg to advance over the bridge.

The battle that follows is not shown. Cueur fights well, but the Black Knight puts him in such dire straits on that narrow bridge that he falls, together with his horse, into the Stream of Tears.

apres quilz neurent pas granment alle quilz se regarderent
et virent deuant eulx vng moult hault pont de fust ctra
uers de la riuiere forble fraesle dancienne facion et estroit
amerueilles Sicque apaine y pouoit passer vng cheual
defront la riuiere estoit creuse et voide durement Sicque d
la voideur deleaue elle faisoit tout croutter et tũbler le pont

Cõment le uer et desir trouuerent le pont ou il se combatit
T de lautre part du pont rauoit vng cheualier
tout arme dunes armes noures fors que sur son
escu qui estoit noir auoit trois fleurs de souffre et estoit

The combat is now over and the Black Knight rides off. Dame Melancholy is gone—in her place there is another lady, Hope *(Esperance)*. It is she who pulls Cueur from the muddy stream, his horse having already scrambled out. In the stream float the broken pieces of Sorrow's lance, but Cueur's lance, too, has fallen into the water. Cueur has tied his shield to his back and is supporting himself on the riverbank with his left arm. Hope is holding her left arm out for balance as she tugs at Cueur's right wrist. Desire bows to her in mute homage, but from the text we learn that he also lends her a hand in her rescue work.

The scene is the same as in the previous illustration, though it has shifted a bit, with the bridge and the hills and trees behind it farther off to the left. This brings more of the stream into the picture, with new trees visible, among them a flourishing willow. The figure of Hope can be seen only from the back, but her violet-blue gown with its graceful folds, her abundant golden hair and crown bring fresh color into the picture, just as her appearance gives the story a fresh impetus.

It seems that Hope has followed the two riders out of concern for their fate. On the way she was able to free young Welcome from the bonds of Jealousy, and send him on his way back to Amour. She herself continued on to the Spring of Chance, where she saw the tracks of their horses, and so arrived just in time at the Dangerous Crossing. Again, she counsels them on the journey ahead: "My children, heed my advice, you will find none better anywhere, I shall always care for you, trust me, for I never lie. . . ." Cueur asks her to stay with them, but she seizes the reins of her horse and suddenly vanishes into thin air.

Comment esperance tire le cuer hors de leaue et dit lacteur

Et quant le cuer se vit de hors sil fust ioyeur ce ne
fait pas ademander et regarda qui estoit celle dame
qui lauoit aide ayssir hors deleaue Si congneut q̃
cestoit dame esperance sa bonne maistresse qui ia autre
fois luy auoit tant fait et enseigne de biens Et adonc le
cueur osta son heaulme de la teste et abaissa la ventaille
et puis Ils sentrebaiserent et sentrefirent tel feste et tel

Cueur and Desire are seen here entering the courtyard of a castle through a well-fortified gate. Inside stands a young girl in a torn red dress that leaves her breasts exposed, while an angry man peers out of an upper window. Beyond the fortress walls and towers a hilly landscape extends into the distance, while in the foreground the Stream of Tears flows past the outer walls.

Hope has told them about this castle and thus prepared them for the experience awaiting them inside it. Though described in the text as sadly decayed, the painting shows the castle as being quite handsome, with a twin-towered entrance gate resembling the famous Porta Nigra in Trier (the chief Roman monument of that ancient German city). The inscription on the gate reads:

> All the inhabitants of the valley below call this the hill of Despondency. It is ruled by Sadness *(Dame Tristesse)* and Wrath *(Lord Courroux)* who has done harm to many a man. . . .

Hungry and tired, the travelers freely enter the unguarded gate. A lance leaning against it is gladly picked up by Cueur, who had lost his own in the struggle with the Black Knight. Meanwhile, the gatekeeper, Sloth *(Paresse)*, has awakened, hastily slipped on her ragged dress, and with her garters still hanging over her shoes, stands screaming in mid-courtyard. This brings the owner to the window above the three-cornered pediment atop the entrance to the tower. Red-faced with anger, he stretches out an accusing hand at the intruders, welcoming them with threats and curses: "How dare you enter here? Who sent you, the Devil? For the shame and injury you bring upon me, you shall pay with your life. . . ."

ordee et deffaucee et les tenoit fessees ensamble deuant son
ventre et sen venoit tout rechignant de despit Et quant elle
vit les deux compaignons qui estoient entres ou chastel elle
se commenca a escrier si merueilleusement quil nest homme qui
nen eust freeur Mais courouer le seigneur du chastel quant
Il lourt fist fermer hastiuement lurs du maistre donior
et mist la teste par vne fenestre et vit les deux compaignons
en my la court / si leur dist en telle maniere

25v

Again there is a shifting of the same scene from the previous setting. The view is from farther to the left and higher up. The entrance gate is no longer visible, but we are looking into the same courtyard over a wall running parallel to the bottom of the frame. This time, a few cracks in the walls and moss and weeds growing in the crevices suggest the decayed state of the property.

A knightly duel has been going on as the splintered lances on the cobblestones show. The two knights on their horses are entangled in close combat, swords swinging. Wrath's shield bears a device of three thistles on a thorny branch. His helmet is a golden dragon's head spewing fire, by some ingenious device, directly at the heart on Cueur's helmet. Desire, hands folded and seated on his horse (which again turns its head away), anxiously observes the combatants from the right.

The second phase of combat is illustrated here. Then the knights dismount and continue fighting on foot in savage fury, causing so much blood to flow that the ground is covered with it, and they can hardly stand up any longer. Finally, Cueur succeeds in splitting Wrath's helmet. At this point the Lady Sorrow comes running out of the castle, to plead for her lord's life. Cueur grants her wish on condition that Wrath promise never again to fight against Love and all his devotees. Sorrow is ugly, but she is a lady, and Cueur feels sorry for her. He asks for a night's lodging and she invites him to follow her into the castle. Carrying a flickering candle, she leads him through a succession of dark rooms until they come to tiny chamber which she bids him enter. Its floor is a trap door, and Cueur falls into a gloomy dungeon beneath. Desire escapes, however, as Sloth is asleep again, and rides out unhindered through the gate.

Compaignie point ne mas abattu
Se ie suis cheu aussi es tu
Or fault quensamble combatons
Et que vng petit nous tastons
Qui mieulx despee frappera
Et qui mieulx sen eschappera
Deable te fist passer le pas
Qui que se fust ne tamoit pas

Icy parle lacteur et dit ainsi que
Quant le cueur se ourt ainsi despriser et rampouner Il
estraint les dens dyre et de mautalant espris et mist

The artist uses a relatively insignificant incident in the romance as an opportunity here to give full, magical play to light and color over the landscape. The dark blue of the night sky is yielding to the radiance of the sun rising just behind the dark-green trees on the hilly horizon fast brightening along its entire length. Only the declivity at left and center still lies in shadow, but the sun's rays already outline the tree trunks of the firs from beneath which Desire has emerged, lighting up his face and clothing as well. The horses cast no shadows as yet, standing below the light, but the trees at right, in the sun, do. A cluster of white, conical tents in the right background also catches the morning sun at that brief moment when the colors begin to awaken from their night's slumber.

Desire has been riding all night to seek help for Cueur. Where the road turns out of the woods he encounters Love's messenger, Modest Plea *(Humble Requeste)*, identified by the three iron-pointed and silver-feathered arrows on a blue shield supported by two angels, which form the heraldic device of the God of Love. Desire and Modest Plea are old acquaintances from Love's court. "Well met!" Desire cries out joyfully. "Sweet friend, what good wind has blown you my way, and whose tents are those beside the stream?"

"It is my Lord Amour who has sent me to bring his friends here, gathered together to fight against the enemies of Love under the leadership of Honor *(Honneur)*. These enemies are Badmouth *(Malle-Bouche)* and Evil Gossips *(Les Medisants)*, at whose orders the villains Denial, Shame, and Fear took the Lady Sweet Grace captive," replies Modest Plea. Hearing this, Desire can hope that the fighting forces of the God of Love will also liberate Cueur.

Icy parle de ſir a humble Requeſte le pourſuuat damouꝛs et dit
Que ſoyez lee tres bien trouue
Gent pourſuiuant bien aprouue
Mon douly amy humble Requeſte
Dittee moy ou allez en queſte

31ᵥ

On his way to Honor's tent, Desire is glad to have found help so soon but sad that Amour has so many enemies, and that the Lady Sweet Grace is being held captive. At Honor's tent he has dismounted, removed his hat, and is down on one knee (his horse, too, is bowing its head in homage). Honor is emerging from his tent, the barons, with whom he has just held council, behind him. They are Renown *(Renom)* and Valor *(Vaillance)*. Desire greets the general respectfully, then reports that one of Amour's most faithful servants has been treacherously captured by the infamous Sorrow, as he was seeking Sweet Grace. He begs Honor to rescue Cueur.

Again, the scene is bright with color, beginning with the low green shrubs in the foreground set off by the lighter green of the bunched grasses. The tents, seen closer-to, with broad borders ornamented in red, green, and gold, finials and fluttering pennants glittering against a strip of blue sky, are resplendent with color, climaxing at the center in Honor's princely patterned red gown trimmed with fur. Honor wears two heron feathers pinned to his hat by a rich jewel. Here, in Amour's tenting ground, there are no shadows; all is light and joyous color.

Honor sends Renown to free Cueur, with the help of Pleasure *(Plaisir)* and Pastime *(Deduit)*, sworn enemies of Wrath and Sadness. They take Wrath's castle by storm and, using ropes, pull Cueur up from his dungeon. He returns with them to Honor's camp, but is anxious to push on immediately so as to free Sweet Grace without further delay. Honor sends Generosity *(Largesse)* along with him as an aide. They spend the night in Renown's tent, hear mass in the morning, then take their leave of Honor.

Lore sacollerent et sentrecommanderent adieu Et sen ala hum
ble requeste diligemment a ses affaires Et de fur fist tant quil
bint auy tantes et pauillons quil auoit beu Si demanda
la tente donneur et affes fut qui la lur moustra Il descen
dit apied et entra enla tente et trouua honneur qui tenoit
conseil auecques ses barons dece quil auoit afaire Et mist
le genoil aterre et le salua en lui disant

Three well-dressed young men stand before a little stone house that has seen better days (to judge by the two slender columns flanking its doorway), its walls now showing deep cracks and loose masonry. A large tablet above the door reads:

> This region vast and drear is called The Plain of Tiresome Brooding
> (*Le Plain de Pensée Ennuyeuse*).

We learn from the text that Grievous Sigh (*Grief Soupir*) plans to bring his unhappy life to an end here.

We instantly recognize Desire and Cueur, wearing his red cap instead of the helmet, his right hand resting familiarly on the shoulder of the man in red, Generosity. The scene is another variation on a favorite subject of the artist: the spectacle of the awakening light. The sun itself has not yet risen, but its first rays are gleaming in the trough between two hills, forcing back the dark blue of the night sky. The painting has few details to distract the viewer from this marvel of light illuminating the sky above the plain, between the figures in the foreground and the hills on the horizon.

On the wide plain only one tall pine stands out, Cueur's lance leaning against it, his helmet and shield at its foot. The three companions had caught sight of this tree the day before and from that moment had ridden straight toward it. They reached it just an hour before midnight, unsaddled their horses to graze at will, then lay down to sleep in the tree's shelter. Next morning, they discovered the little house of Grievous Sigh. Now they enter and meet the old man, pale and thin, with a long beard. He has nothing to give them but some inedible bread, and they too begin to sigh grievously.

Icy parle lacteur et dit ainsi que

Quant les trois compaignons eurent leues et ouyes
les lettres qui estoient escriptes ou tableau Ilz
furent pensifz trop durement et se regarderent
lun lautre comme tous esbahis achief de piece le cueur qui
plus estoit beaulx que nulz des autres saula et entra
en la maisonnette le premier et ses deux compaignons
entrerent apres mais Ilz trouverent povre hostel et mal
acoustre Ilz marcherent Jusques au fouyer de la maisonnette

After leaving this plain of sighs the three companions come to a forest they cross in a day's riding, emerging from the woods as evening falls. This time it is the blaze of color around the sinking sun that inspires the artist. The great disk is still visible but enveloped in golden mist. The horizon is dipped in flames, and against this background some clouds are only dark while others are rimmed in red or gold. This is the one painting which shows dark clouds in the sky, where they set off the play of light most effectively. Only the upper part of Cueur's lance and the rim of the Chapel's roof are still gilded by the sunlight. Everything else is in deep shadow, spreading forward from the dark, distant mountains on the horizon. The red of Cueur's saddle, Generosity's tunic, and the heart on the helmet is subdued; even Desire's white garb is grayed over, here. All three are exhausted from their long ride. Generosity's stallion is relieving himself in the discreet dusk.

The chapel they are facing is part of a hermitage. The hermit inside has just finished his evening prayers and kindly agrees to let them stay the night, but warns them that he already has one guest, a noble lady, whose permission he must obtain before accepting additional guests. The lady turns out to be none other than Hope. They greet each other with delight and recount their separate adventures. The hermit prepares a meal for them, provides for the horses, and gives them bedding for the night. In the morning the hermit reads them the Mass of the Holy Ghost, at their joint request. Again Cueur asks Hope for advice and again she gives it, then vanishes as suddenly as she did before.

face a raconter Jusques ace quilz vindrent pres de celuy
boys mais Ilz ny peurent pas si tost venir que le souleil
ne fust couche auant quilz y arriuassent Et quant Ilz
furent la arriuez Ilz regarderent deuant eulx et virent
aloree du boys vng petit hermitaige Ilz turent celle part
et descendirent de dessus leurs cheuaulx et entrerent en la
chappelle de lermitaige la ou Ilz trouuerent lermite disant
ses complies Ilz le saluerent et luy demanderent a herber
gier pour celle nuyt et lermite qui bien preudome ses
sembloit leur respondit disant en telle maniere

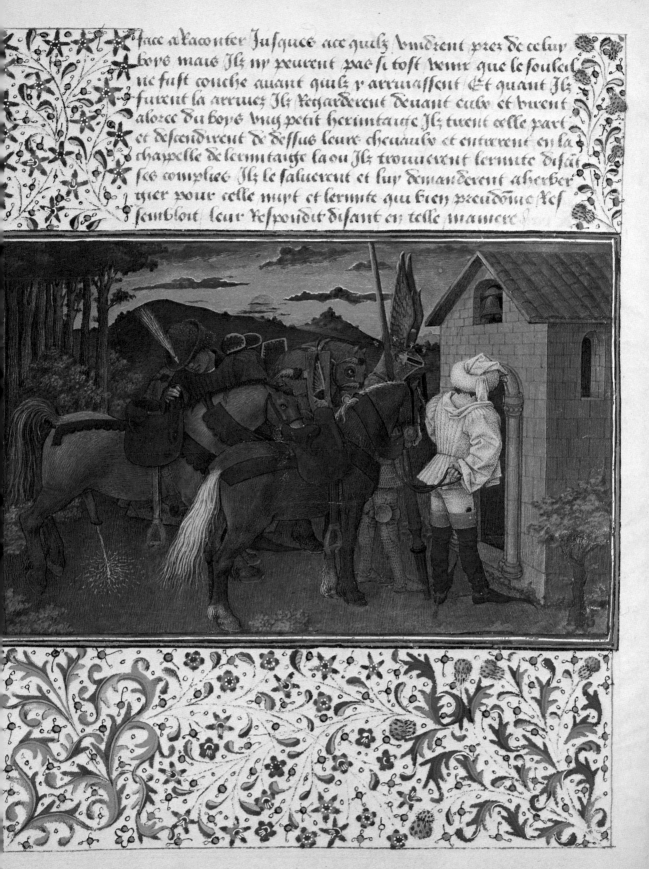

47v

Hope has told Cueur that they will soon reach the seacoast, where a ship will be waiting to transport them to the Isle of Love. The gray-green, shimmering expanse of the sea provides a new backdrop for the bright colors in the foreground, ending at the top with the sharp line of the horizon, beyond which only the pale blue sky and ice-blue distant mountains are visible.

This scene is the most heavily populated of all—somehow, each of the knights has acquired a page of his own. Cueur's page has already removed his lord's spurs and looks on as Cueur sets foot on the boat, characteristically the first to do so. Generosity has set his left foot on a rock to let his page remove his second spur, and Desire's valet stands beside him, holding both spurs in his hand. Only two horses are in view, pawing the ground; with their neighing, they have awakened the two young women who had been asleep in the boat: Confidante *(Fiance)* and Accord *(Entente)*, serving ladies at Amour's court, charged with bringing the lover to the island castle of the God of Love. The sail is still furled, the oars lying ready in the boat. Despite their modish court dress, the girls are quite capable and smilingly decline the assistance offered by Cueur and Desire.

On the yellow sands of the beach, seashells and rocks lie scattered. Some large rocks at the right appear to be under water. Astern in the water lies a dark object—an anchor?

Icy parle lacteur et dit amsi que
Ces parolles le cueur Incontinent mist pict aterre
tout courroce et bergongneur de ce que tant lauoit
amc et marcha droit ala mer et entra en la naf
selle et ses deux autres compaignons furent Incontinent amsi
et habandonnerent tous leurs cheuaulx aleurs varletz qui
les prirent et ses emmenent pour le guerredon de leure ser

In this extraordinary night scene, all colors have been muted. Except for the faint gleam of metal from Cueur's armor and Desire's tunic, all clothing has turned black, setting off the barely distinguishable faces and hands in the uncertain light. Ahead in the threatening dark, the jagged reefs of a rocky island are discernible; beyond its distant outline there is the pale hint of an as yet invisible moon. The night sky is full of golden stars. Waves are beating against the reefs which the stern of the boat is approaching. At the edge of the cliff, two women are seen angling; one is just lifting her catch out of the water. Sociability *(Compaignie)* and Friendship *(Amittié)* are good friends of Confidante and Accord. Their rocky island is a way station on the voyage to the Isle of Love; their tent shows a little light at the top; they are here to offer friendly hospitality to lovers en route.

The crossing was stormy; all three companions were struck down by seasickness. Cared for by the crew (Confidante and Accord), Cueur, Desire, and Generosity fell asleep toward evening as the storm abated, and slept until they reached the island. Here they now land and are invited into the tent by their hostesses. Instead of bread they are served a kind of biscuit made of roasted fish, called Farewell *(Validire),* and a salad, Sweet Reply *(Doulce Response).* It is Friday and thus a fast day, on which no other food may be eaten in Love's domain. Served with an excellent wine, the meal is gratefully received, the hardships forgotten. After the repast everyone goes outdoors, Sociability and Friendship to take up their fishing rods again, because the fish can be caught only at night. The guests wander about the island admiring the waves glittering in the light of the stars, under the night sky.

Jcy parle lacteur et dit ainsi que fflanceff
Donecques deseendirent les babaffeurs premiere et
les dames marinieres apres et compaignie et amit
rie les Receurent en leur cabane Joyeufement et de
treffon voulou et les furent mengier dece que pour lors Ik
xpnoyent auoir la Ceftaffauoir en lieu de pain biscuyt du
poiffon roufty lequel Ik appelloient entre eulx validire Se

BIBLIOGRAPHY

Early, very comprehensive and exhaustive scholarly works on René show no awareness of the existence of the Vienna manuscript:

Villeneuve Bargemont, L. F. de: *Histoire de René d-Anjou.* 3 vols. Paris, 1825.

Quatrebarbes (ed.): *Oeuvres completes du Roi René.* 4 vols. Angers, 1845–46.

Lecoy de la Marche, A.: *Le Roi René.* 2 vols. Paris, 1875.

The first publication on the Vienna manuscript was:

Waagen, G. F.: *Die vornehmsten Kunstdenkmäler in Wien* (The Most Distinguished Works of Art in Vienna—tr.). 2 vols. Vienna, 1867, pp. 83 ff.

But Durrieu was the first to draw the attention of French and then all art historians, worldwide, to the significance of this manuscript:

Durrieu, P.: "Notes sur quelques manuscrits françaises ou d'origine française conservés dans des Bibliothèques d'Allemagne." In: Bibliothèque de l'Ecole des Chartes, vol. 53. Paris, 1892, pp. 138 ff.

Since then the literature on the subject has grown almost beyond all bounds. The most important publications are, in chronological order:

Champion, P.: *Le roi René écrivain.* Monaco, 1925.

Smital, O. and Winkler, E.: *Livre du Cuer d'amours espris.* Einleitungs und Textband zur Faksimile-Augsgabe. Vienna, 1926.

Trenkler, E.: *Das Livre du cuer d'amours espris des Herzogs René d' Anjou.* Vienna, 1946.

Chamson, A. (ed.): *Le Livre du coeur d'amour epris du Roi René.* Paris, 1949.

Levron, J.: *La vie et les moeurs du bon roi René.* Paris, 1953.

Pächt, O.: "René d'Anjou et les Van Eyck." In: *Cahiers de l'Association des Etudes Françaises.* Paris, 1956, pp. 41–76.

Quarré, P.: "Le Roi René, prisonnier du duc de Bourgogne et son oeuvre de peintre." In: *La revue du Louvre.* Paris, 1964, pp. 67–74.

Pächt, O.: René d'Anjou-Studien, I. In: *Jahrbuch der kunsthistorischen Sammlungen in Wien*, 69 (1973), pp. 39–88.

Pächt, O. and Thoss, D.: *Die illuminierten Handschriften und Inkunabeln der österreichischen National Bibliothek.* Französische Schule I. Vienna, 1974, pp. 37–48.